JOHN CORIGLIANO

T0051151

STRING QUARTET

(Full Score)

ED 4028
Corrected Printing: April 2019

ISBN 978-0-7935-7427-8

G. SCHIRMER, Inc.

DISTRIBUTED BY

7777 W. BLUEMOUND RD. P.O. BOX 13819 MILWAUKEE, WI 53213

Contact us:
Hal Leonard
7777 West Bluemound Road
Milwaukee, WI 53213
Email: info@halleonard.com

In Europe, contact:
Hal Leonard Europe Limited
42 Wigmore Street
Marylebone, London, W1U 2RN
Email: info@halleonardeurope.com

In Australia, contact:
Hal Leonard Australia Pty. Ltd.
4 Lentara Court
Cheltenham, Victoria, 3192 Australia
Email: info@halleonard.com.au

* movements IV. and V. are played without pause.

In writing my string quartet I was always aware that I was dealing with a unique instrument (composed of four instrumentalists). Unlike the orchestra (unified by a maestro's vision and beat) or most other chamber combinations (composed of highly differentiated soloists), the string quartet must be able to produce a conductorless unity of sound and ensemble that can only be accomplished by years of playing together.

It is possible to ask a quartet to play and "breathe" as one instrument, even while employing considerable rhythmic freedom (rubato). Alternately, the players can achieve an independence from one another that is otherwise only possible when a group is precisely conducted. These special qualities of quartet playing became the basis of my first essay in this extraordinary medium.

Added to this was the fact that I was writing for one of the greatest of all quartets, the Cleveland Quartet, and that they were presenting this work during their farewell concert tour before disbanding. The idea of an ensemble such as this playing for the last time surely colored the emotional palate of my quartet with a feeling of farewell, and while the work is basically abstract in content, certain areas (like the final Postlude) cannot help but echo these sentiments.

Architecturally, the 35-minute work is in five movements that bear a superficial resemblance to the arch-form principles of Bartok's fourth quartet (movements I and V are related and movements II and IV are related, with III as a central "night music"), but in fact all five movements of the quartet are also united by similar motives and thematic content. Specifically, the quartet is based upon a motto composed of even repetitions of a single tone, and a sequence of disjunct minor thirds. There are also four pitch centers recurring throughout the work: C, C-sharp, G and G-sharp.

I. Prelude

This short movement utilizes two kinds of muted playing. It opens and closes using a "practice mute" (which reduces the sound to a whisper) while the central section employs a standard sordino. Threads of sound gently appear from and disappear into silence. They have an unfocused and ambient feel because each of the players is playing very slightly out of synchronization with the others.

Gradually the texture becomes clearer, and the basic elements of the quartet are introduced: two of the pitch centers (G and C-sharp), the disjunct minor thirds (here ascending), and a serene chordal fragment based upon the repeated single- tone motive. The movement ends as the ascending thirds disappear into silence.

II. Scherzo

Slashing evenly-repeated chords begin the movement and are counterpoised against suddenly-faster irreverent "pop"-ish asides. Variants of the repeated-note motive lead to a virtuoso passage in which all four players articulate in rapid 16th-notes both the repeated single tones and the disjunct minor thirds. A recapitulation of the slashing chords leads to a gentle trio: a chaconne based upon the chordal fragments in the prelude is played by a duo, while the other two players provide lyrical counterpoint. A return to the opening chords and an even larger and wilder recapitulation of earlier material brings the movement to a frenetic end.

III. Nocturne

Some years ago during a vacation in Morocco, I stayed at the Palais Jamais in Fez. My room overlooked the old city and during the night (about 4 a.m.) I was awakened by the calls of the muezzins from the many mosques in the city. First one, then another, and finally dozens of independent calls created a glorious counterpoint, and at one moment all of the calls held on to a single note (pure accident) and the result was a major chord. The calls died away, a cock crowed and a dog barked to announce the sun.

This Nocturne recalls that memory—the serenity of the Moroccan night, the calls (here composed of motivic fragments of repeated notes and minor thirds) and the descent to silence and the dawn.

IV. Fugue

I have always been fascinated by counterpoint. In this process a theme set against a steady beat is given a highly individual rhythmic profile with long notes, short notes and syncopations, so that when it is played against other material its line will stand out clearly. An opposing theme, also set against this same steady beat, will have a different rhythmic profile; it will rest when the first theme plays and vice versa. This enables us to hear both themes independently, note against note.

I always wondered if voices could be made independent by exactly the opposite method: the themes would all be composed of even beats, with absolutely no rhythmic profile. Instead of both themes set against a common beat (which would result in chords) each voice would travel at a different speed (or tempo). The misalignment that occurs when two rhythmically identical themes travel at two different speeds (say, 60 versus 72 beats per minute) would separate them as surely as syncopation does within a common beat.

The problem comes in trying to execute such a technique. One cannot simply instruct the players to play at these different tempi, for it is impossible to sustain them precisely for any length of time. Therefore, these independent lines must be accurately notated in a common rhythm, even though they are not heard that way. While this is difficult to play, it is not hard to hear; listen for example to the opening viola subject answered by a slightly slower second violin while the viola continues at its own tempo.

The movement is marked "severe," and there is a starkness to this music brought about not only by the dissonant material {the subject is composed of both the repeated tone and the disjunct minor thirds, this time descending) , but also by the total independence of the voices. They seem to travel alone, unrelated to each other, yet identical to each other.

There are two sections in the Fugue where the four instruments unite in a common rhythm. This is usually accomplished by one or another of the instruments "catching up" with the others. Other elements include asynchronous "chases" in the upper three strings and a serene {and synchronous) slow section. Formally the Fugue is traditional, with an exposition, central section and strettoed recapitulation.

V. Postlude The ending of the Fugue is joined to the Postlude. In this movement, the lower three strings are spatially offset by the first violin which enters, muted, on the highest C-sharp. The distance between the solo violin and the rest of the quartet remains vast in this first section, which also introduces a cadence derived from the Prelude and the trio of the Scherzo. An ornamental recitative-like section in the lower three strings follows, and in time the first violin joins them in a unity of playing. This highly free section, in which all four players play in unison with interspersed chords, demands that the quartet play exactly together, in spite of the music's constantly changing tempo.

An impassioned climax leads to a long descending passage, after which the texture of single-line playing returns. This gradually changes into the asynchronous ambient-sounding threads of the first movement, and with the addition of practice mutes and an exact retrograde of the opening music, the quartet fades into silence.

— John Corigliano

The String Quartet was commissioned by the Lincoln Center for the Performing Arts for the Cleveland Quartet.

The first performance was by the Cleveland Quartet on October 26, 1995, at the St. Lawrence Centre for the Arts in Toronto.

It has been recorded by the Cleveland Quartet on Telarc CD-80415, "The Farewell Recording."

This recording received two "Grammy" Awards in 1996:

Best Contemporary Classical Composition and Best Chamber Music Performance.

Duration: ca. 33 minutes

A set of parts is available for purchase (50482921).

STRING QUARTET

I. Prelude

John Corigliano

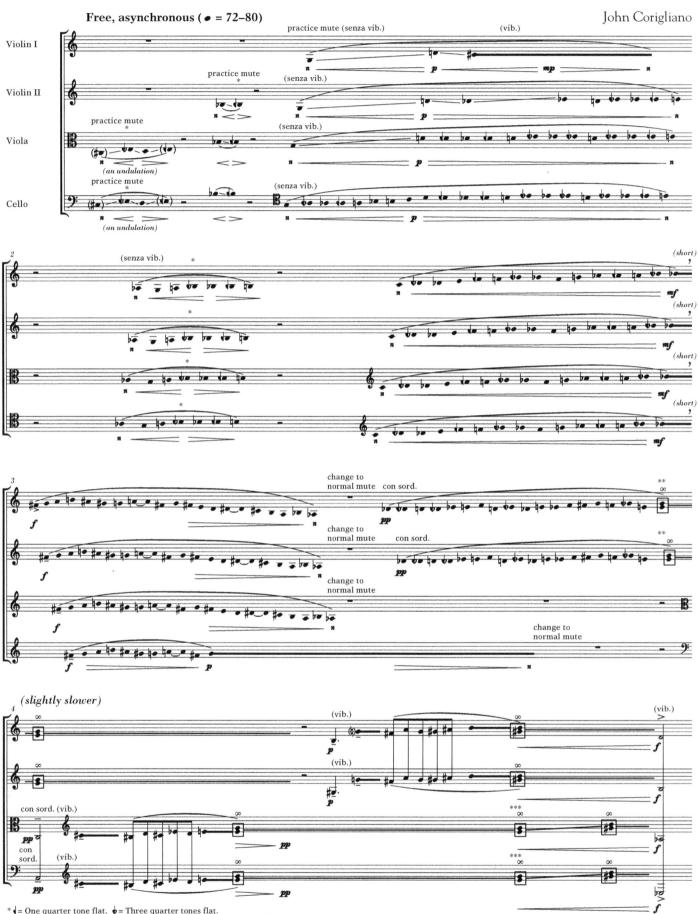

* ♩ = One quarter tone flat. ♭ = Three quarter tones flat.
** Continue "noodling," utilizing a variety of intervals (quarter tone flat, three quarter tones flat, half tone, whole tone).
   within and including the two indicated pitches.
*** Continue "noodling," maintaining a minor third as the extreme ranges. Very slowly ascend, maintaining the minor third.

(♩ = ca. 69)

* In a similar manner.
** Expand to a distance of a minor third. Continue playing freely while ascending and keeping the general pitch range of a minor third.

II. Scherzo

* Non-pitched.

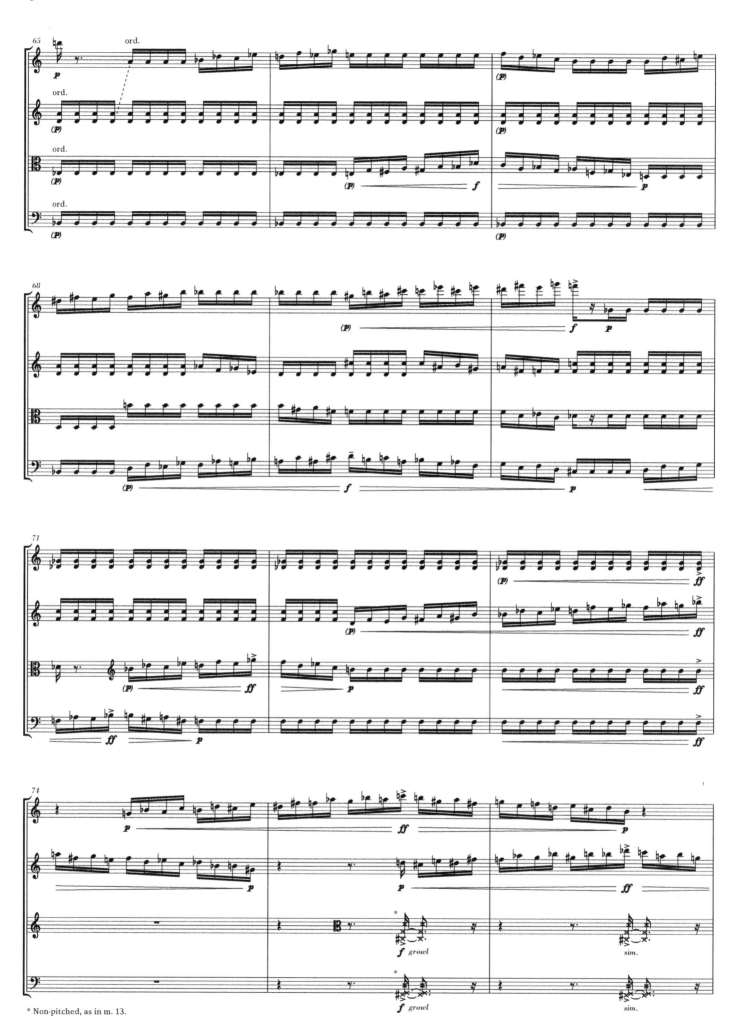

* Non-pitched, as in m. 13.

* E♮ optional.

* Due to the practice mute, Violin II must play louder than Viola to maintain dynamic balance.

* While preserving the interval of a minor 3rd, very slowly move upwards (slow glissando), always articulating the 16th-note rhythm. The minor 3rds will climb upwards.

* While preserving the interval of a minor 3rd, very slowly move upwards (slow glissando), always articulating the 16th-note rhythm. The minor 3rds will climb upwards.

* Ascending minor-3rd pattern continues from approximately where it left off.

III. Nocturne

Improvisatory, free ♩ = ca. 46

* Glissando into new pitch level, no crescendo.

* Play each figure enclosed in the box sequentially. Then vary the order of the figures. Sing freely and individually.

IV. Fugue

Severe ♩ = ca. 72

* Brackets indicate implied measures, e.g.:

* Violins cut off abruptly when Cello and Viola enter.
** Bring out melody.
*** Violins and Viola cut off abruptly when Cello enters.

* Violins and Viola play pianissimo, sul ponticello, as fast as possible. Each player should "chase" the other, with Violin I initiating the chase. The players should be asynchronous. Play the indicated octave changes (shown in brackets) on the repeat.

* One by one, align rhythms, finish repetitions, and settle on G. But do not take too long!
** Slow down evenly so that at measure 85, each part is aligned with the cello.
*** Emphasize grace notes.

* Optional 8va bassa.

* Notes in parentheses are optional.

* Ossia, measure 147, Vn. I plays Vn. II and Vn. II plays Vn. I.
** "Chase" asynchronously, as in measure 88.

* Continue even legatissimo pulses, with gradual rallentando and diminuendo.

attacca

V. Postlude

* 𝅘 = One quarter tone flat. 𝅘 = Three quarter tones flat.

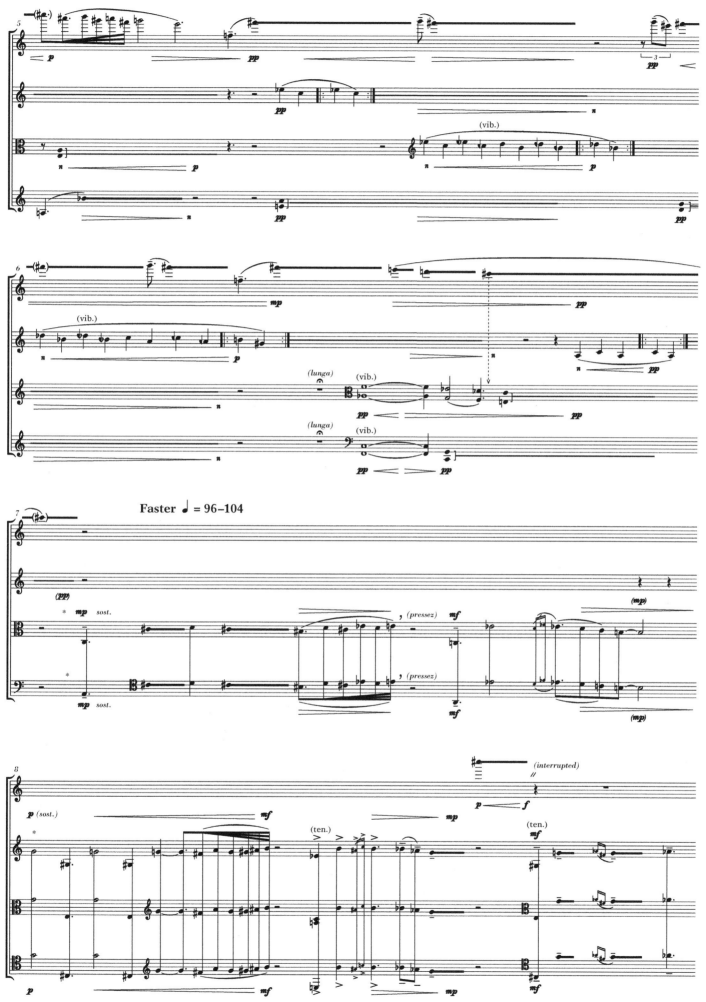

Faster ♩ = 96–104

* Passages stemmed together must be played very freely and yet *exactly* together.

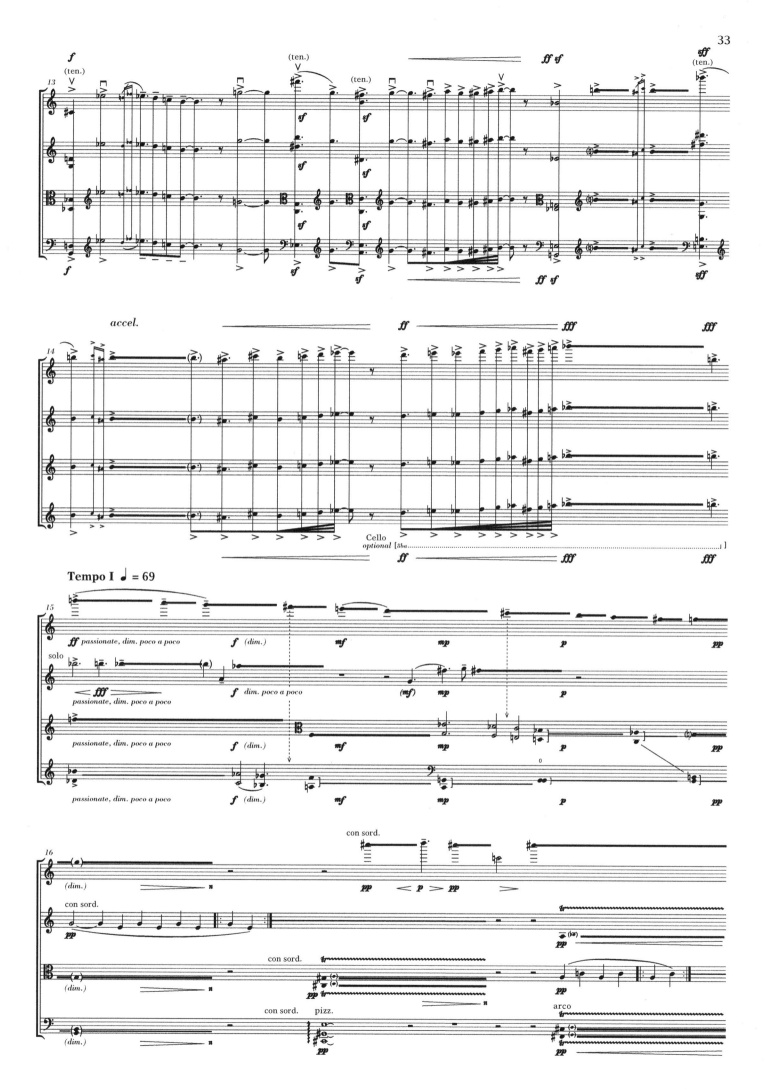

34

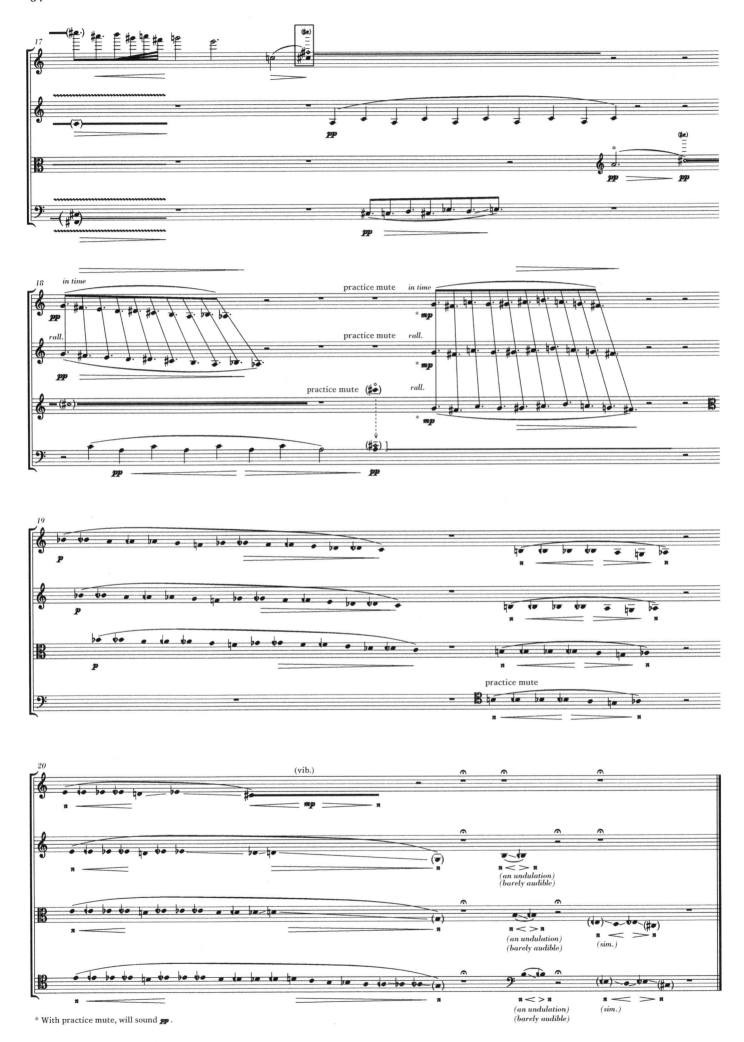

* With practice mute, will sound *pp* .